EDUCATION OF WOMEN

This edition published by Lector House in 2024

ISBN: 978-93-6138-724-1
Edition copyright © 2024 by Lector House LLP
All rights reserved under the International Copyright Conventions.

Every possible effort has been made to ensure that the information contained in this book is accurate at the time of going to press and the publisher cannot accept responsibility for any errors or omissions, however caused, in this unabridged, slightly corrected republication of the text of the first edition. No responsibility for loss or damage occasioned to any person, acting or refraining from action, as a result of the material in this publication can be accepted by the publisher. The publisher is not associated with any product or vendor mentioned in the book. The contents of this work are intended to further general scientific research, understanding and discussion, only. Readers should consult with a specialist, where appropriate.

No part of this publication may be reproduced, stored in a retrieval system, or transmitted, in any form, or by any means, electronic, mechanical, photocopying or otherwise, without the prior permission of the publisher.

Lector House LLP
Registered Office: H. No. 96, Block C, Tomar Colony,
Burari, Delhi – 110084, India
info@lectorhouse.com
www.lectorhouse.com

EDUCATION OF WOMEN

MARTHA CAREY THOMAS,
NICHOLAS MURRAY BUTLER

2024

LECTOR HOUSE LLP

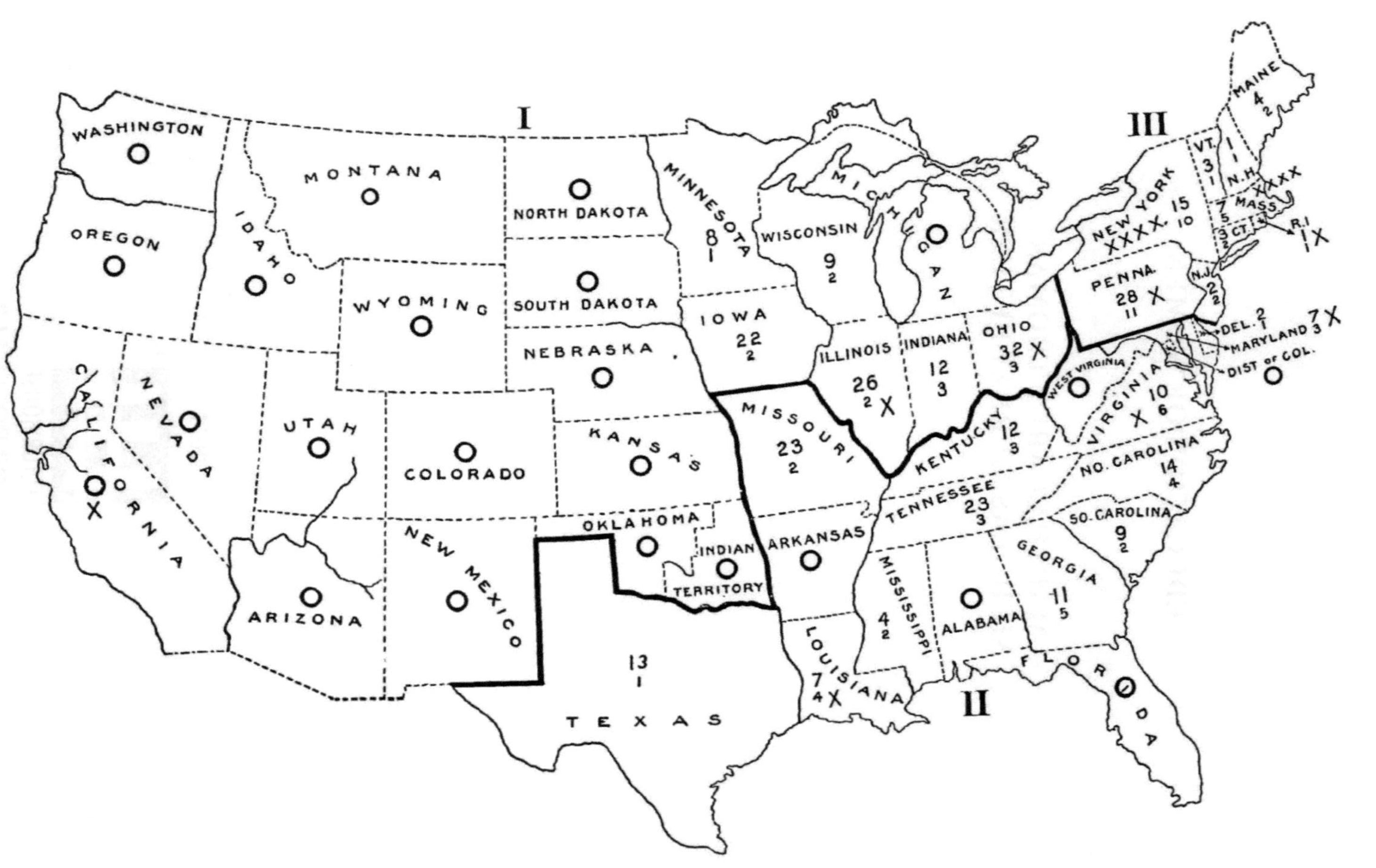

I
II
III
WASHINGTON
OREGON
CALIFORNIA
IDAHO
NEVADA
MONTANA
WYOMING
UTAH
ARIZONA
COLORADO
NEW MEXICO
NORTH DAKOTA
SOUTH DAKOTA
NEBRASKA
KANSAS
OKLAHOMA
INDIAN TERRITORY
TEXAS 13 1
MINNESOTA 8 1
IOWA 22 2
MISSOURI 23 2
ARKANSAS
LOUISIANA 7 4
WISCONSIN 9 2
MICHIGAN
ILLINOIS 26 2
INDIANA 12 3
OHIO 32 3
KENTUCKY 12 3
TENNESSEE 23 3
MISSISSIPPI 4 2
ALABAMA
GEORGIA 11 5
FLORIDA
SO. CAROLINA 9 2
NO. CAROLINA 14 4
VIRGINIA 10 6
WEST VIRGINIA
PENNA. 28 11
NEW YORK 15 10
N.J. 2 2
DEL. 2 1
MARYLAND 7 3
DIST. of COL.
VT. 3 1
N.H. 1 1
MAINE 4 2
MASS. 7 5
CT. 3 2
R.I. 1 1

Attitude of different sections of the United States toward coeducation and separate education of men and women

O = No colleges in state closed to women.

Upper figure = number coeducational colleges and colleges for men only in state, exclusive of Roman Catholic colleges.

Lower figure = colleges in state closed to women.

X = independent or affiliated colleges for women.

In this table are included all the colleges (except Roman Catholic colleges) given in the U. S. ed. rep. for 1897–98.

Section I = 20 western states and 4 territories.

Section II = 14 southern and 2 southern middle states and District of Columbia.

Section III = 6 New England states and 3 northern middle states.

DEPARTMENT OF EDUCATION
FOR THE
UNITED STATES COMMISSION TO THE PARIS EXPOSITION OF 1900

*　　*　　*　　*　　*

MONOGRAPHS ON EDUCATION IN THE UNITED STATES

EDITED BY

NICHOLAS MURRAY BUTLER

Professor of Philosophy and Education in Columbia University, New York

EDUCATION OF WOMEN

BY

M. CAREY THOMAS

President of Bryn Mawr College, Bryn Mawr, Pennsylvania

EDUCATION OF WOMEN

The higher education of women in America is taking place before our eyes on a vast scale and in a variety of ways. Every phase of this great experiment, if experiment we choose to call it, may be studied almost simultaneously. Women are taking advantage of all the various kinds of education offered them in great and ever-increasing numbers, and the period of thirty years, or thereabouts, that has elapsed since the beginning of the movement is sufficient to authorize us in drawing certain definite conclusions. The higher education of women naturally divides itself into college education designed primarily to train the mental faculties by means of a liberal education, and only secondarily, to equip the student for self-support, and professional or special education, directed primarily toward one of the money-making occupations.

College Education

Women's college education is carried on in three different classes of institutions: coeducational colleges, independent women's colleges and women's colleges connected more or less closely with some one of the colleges for men.

1. Coeducation—Coeducation is the prevailing system of college education in the United States for both men and women. In the western states and territories it is almost the only system of education, and it is rapidly becoming the prevailing system in the south, where the influence of the state universities is predominant. On the other hand, in the New England

and middle states the great majority of the youth of both sexes are still receiving a separate college education. Coeducation was introduced into colleges in the west as a logical consequence of the so-called American system of free elementary and secondary schools. During the great school revival of 1830–45 and the ensuing years until the outbreak of the civil war in 1861, free elementary and secondary schools were established throughout New England and the middle states and such western states as existed in those days. It was a fortunate circumstance for girls that the country was at that time sparsely settled; in most neighborhoods it was so difficult to establish and secure pupils for even one grammar school and one high school that girls were admitted from the first to both[1]. In the reorganization of lower and higher education that took place between 1865 and 1870 this same system, bringing with it the complete coeducation of the sexes, was introduced throughout the south both for whites and negroes, and was extended to every part of the west. In no part of the country, except in a few large eastern cities, was any distinction made in elementary or secondary education between boys and girls[2]. The second fortunate and in

[1] That their admission was due in large part to the stress of circumstances is shown by the fact that in the very states in which these coeducational schools had been established there was manifested on other occasions a most illiberal attitude toward girls' education. In the few cities of the Atlantic seaboard, where European conservatism was too strong to allow girls to be taught with boys in the new high schools, and where there were boys enough to fill the schools, girls had to wait much longer before their needs were provided for at all, and then most inadequately. In Boston, where the boys' and girls' high schools were separated, it was impossible until 1878 for a Boston girl to be prepared for college in a city high school, whereas, in the country towns of Massachusetts, where boys and girls were taught together in the high schools, the girl had had the same opportunities as the boy for twenty-five or thirty years. Indeed, it was not until 1852 that Boston girls obtained, and then only in connection with the normal school, a public high-school education of any kind whatsoever. In Philadelphia, where boys and girls are taught separately in the high schools, no girl could be prepared for college before 1893, neither Latin, French, nor German being taught in the girls' high school, whereas, for many years the boys' high school had prepared boys for college. In Baltimore the two girls' high schools are still, in 1900, unable to prepare girls for college, whereas the boys' high school has for years prepared boys to enter the Johns Hopkins university. The impossibility of preparing girls for college is only another way of stating that the instruction given is very imperfect.

[2] The magnitude of this fact will be apparent if we reflect that here for the first time the girls of a great nation, especially of the poorer classes, have from their earliest infancy to the age of eighteen or nineteen received the same education as the boys, and that the ladder leading, in Huxley's words, from the gutter to the university may be climbed as easily by a girl as by a boy. Although college education has affected as yet only a very few out of the great number of adult women in the United States, the free opportunities for secondary education have influenced the whole American people for nearly two-thirds of a

like manner almost accidental factor in the education of American women was the occurrence of the civil war at the formative period of the public schools, with the result of placing the elementary and secondary education of both boys and girls overwhelmingly in the hands of women teachers. In no other country of the world has this ever been the case, and its influence upon women's education has been very great. The five years of the civil war, which drained all the northern and western states of men, caused women teachers to be employed in the public and private schools in large numbers, and in the first reports of the national bureau of education, organized after the war, we see that there were already fewer men than women teaching in the public schools of the United States. This result proved not to be temporary, but permanent, and from 1865 until the present time not only the elementary teaching of boys and girls but the secondary education of both has been increasingly in the hands of women[3]. When most of the state universities of the west were founded they were in reality scarcely more than secondary schools supplemented, in most cases, by large preparatory departments. Girls were already being educated with boys in all the high schools of the west, and not to admit them to the state universities would have been to break with tradition. Women were also firmly established as teachers in the secondary schools and it was patent to all thoughtful men that they must be given opportunities for higher education, if only for the sake of the secondary education of the boys of the country.[4] The development

century. The men of the poorer classes have had, as a rule, mothers as well educated as their fathers, indeed, better educated; to this, more than to any other single cause, I think, may be attributed what by other nations is regarded as the phenomenal industrial progress of the United States. Our commercial rivals could probably take no one step that would so tend to place them on a level with American competition as to open to girls without distinction all their elementary and secondary schools for boys. In 1892, girls formed 55.9 per cent, and in 1898, 56.5 per cent of all pupils in the public and private secondary schools of the United States.

[3] In 1870 women formed 59.0 per cent; in 1880, 57.2 per cent; in 1890, 65.5 per cent; and in 1898, 67.8 per cent (in the North Atlantic Division 80.8 per cent) of all teachers in the public elementary and secondary schools of the United States (U. S. ed. rep. for 1897–98, pp. xiii, lxxv). It has been frequently remarked that the feminine pronouns "she" and "her" are instinctively used in America in common speech with reference to a teacher. Moreover more women than men are teaching in the public and private secondary schools of the United States (in 1898, women formed 53.8 per cent of the total number of secondary teachers, see U. S. ed. rep. for 1897–98, pp. 2053, 2069); whereas in all other countries the secondary teaching of boys is wholly in the hands of men.

[4] In many cases in the west women made their way into the universities through the normal department of the university, being admitted to that first of all. The summer schools of western colleges, chiefly attended by teachers, among whom women were in

of women's education in the east has followed a different course because there were in the east no state universities, and the private colleges for men had been founded before women were suffered to become either pupils or teachers in schools. The admission of women to the existing eastern colleges was, therefore, as much an innovation as it would have been in Europe. The coeducation of men and women in colleges, and at the same time the college education of women, began in Ohio, the earliest settled of the western states. In 1833 Oberlin collegiate institute (not chartered as a college until 1850) was opened, admitting from the first both men and women. Oberlin was at that time, and is now, hampered by maintaining a secondary school as large as its college department, but it was the first institution for collegiate instruction in the United States where large numbers of men and women were educated together, and the uniformly favorable testimony of its faculty had great influence on the side of coeducation. In 1853 Antioch college, also in Ohio, was opened, and admitted from the beginning men and women on equal terms. Its first president, Horace Mann, was one of the most brilliant and energetic educational leaders in the United States, and his ardent advocacy of coeducation, based on his own practical experience, had great weight with the public.[5] From this time on it became a custom, as state universities were opened in the far west, to admit women. Utah, opened in 1850, Iowa, opened in 1856, Washington, opened in 1862, Kansas, opened in 1866, Minnesota, opened in 1868, and Nebraska, opened in 1871, were coeducational from the outset. Indiana, opened as early as 1820, admitted women in 1868. The state University of Michigan was, at this time, the most important western university, and the only western university well known in the east before the war. When, in 1870, it opened its doors to women, they were for the first time in America admitted to instruction of true college grade. The step was taken in response to public sentiment, as shown by two requests of the state legislature, against the will of the faculty as a whole. The example of the University of Michigan was quickly followed by all the other state universities of the west. In the same year women were allowed to enter the state universities of Illinois and California; in 1873 the only remaining state university closed to women, that of Ohio, admitted them. Wisconsin which, since 1860, had given some instruction to women, became in 1874 unreservedly coeducational. All the state universities of the west,

---

the majority, served also as an entering wedge. (See Woman's work in America, Holt & Co., 1891, pp. 71–75.)

[5] Antioch college opened, however, with only 8 students in its college department, all the rest, 142, belonging to its secondary school.

organized since 1871, have admitted women from the first. In the twenty states which, for convenience, I shall classify as western, there are now twenty state universities open to women, and, in four territories, Arizona, Oklahoma, Indiana and New Mexico, the one university of each territory is open to women. Of the eleven state universities of the southern states the two most western admitted women first, as was to be expected. Missouri became coeducational as early as 1870, and the University of Texas was opened in 1883 as a coeducational institution. Mississippi admitted women in 1882, Kentucky in 1889, Alabama in 1893, South Carolina in 1894, North Carolina in 1897, but only to women prepared to enter the junior and senior years, West Virginia in 1897.[6] The state universities of Virginia, Georgia and Louisiana are still closed. The one state university existing outside the west and south, that of Maine, admitted women in 1872.

The greater part of the college education of the United States, however, is carried on in private, not in state universities. In 1897 over 70 per cent of all the college students in the United States were studying in private colleges, so that for women's higher education their admission to private colleges is really a matter of much greater importance. The part taken by Cornell university in New York state in opening private colleges to women was as significant as the part taken by Michigan in opening state universities. Cornell is in a restricted sense a state university, inasmuch as part of its endowment, like that of the state universities, is derived from state and national funds. Nevertheless, there is little reason to suppose that Cornell would have admitted women had it not been for the generosity of Henry W. Sage, who offered to build and endow a large hall of residence for women at Cornell university. After carefully investigating coeducation in all the institutions where it then existed, and especially in Michigan, the trustees of the university admitted women in 1872. The example set by Cornell was followed very slowly by the other private colleges of the New England and middle states. For the next twenty years the colleges in this section of the United States admitting women might be counted on the fingers of one hand. In Massachusetts Boston university opened its department of arts in 1873, and admitted women to it from the first; but no college for men followed the example of Boston until 1883, when the Massachusetts institute of technology, the most important technical and scientific school in the state, and one of the most important in the United States, admitted

[6] In every case I give the date when full coeducation was introduced; West Virginia, for example, admitted women to limited privileges in 1889.

women. This school, like Cornell, is supported in part from state and national funds. Very recently, in 1892, Tufts college was opened to women. In the west and south the case is different, and the list of private colleges that one after another have become coeducational is too long to be inserted here. Among new coeducational foundations the most important are, on the Pacific coast, the Leland Stanford junior university, opened in 1891, and, in the middle west, Chicago university, opened in 1892. To show the differing attitude toward coeducation of the different sections of the United States, I have arranged the 480 coeducational colleges and separate colleges for men given in the U.S. education report for 1897–98 in a table on the opposite page. In matters like women's education, which are powerfully affected by prejudice and conservative opinion, we find not only a sharp cleavage in opinion and practice between the west and the east of the United States, but also distinct phases of differing opinion, corresponding in the main to the old geographical division of the states into New England, middle, southern and western.[7]

[7] In discussing coeducation I shall, therefore, disregard the divisions into north Atlantic, south Atlantic, north central, south central and western, employed by the U. S. census and the U. S. bureau of education. The New England, middle and southern states are all, of course, eastern, and, with the exception of Vermont, West Virginia, Kentucky, Tennessee and Missouri, are all seaboard states, Pennsylvania being counted as a seaboard state on account of its close river connection with the sea. It will be noted that the inland southern states are rather western than eastern in their characteristics. The northern middle states belong on the whole by their sympathies to New England, the southern middle to the southern states. Missouri, having been a slave state and settled largely by southerners, is still southern in feeling. The District of Columbia also may conveniently be counted with the southern states.

I. *20 western states and 3 territories*			
STATES	Total no. cols.	Coed.	Men only
Ohio	35	29	3 R. C., 1 Luth., 1 P. E., Western reserve.
Indiana	14	9	2 R. C., 1 Luth., 1 Cong., Wabash college.
Illinois	31	24	5 R. C., 1 Ger. Ev., Illinois college.
Michigan	11	10	1 R. C.
Wisconsin	10	7	1 R. C., 1 Luth., 1 Dutch Reformed.
Minnesota	9	7	1 R. C., 1 Luth.
Iowa	22	20	2 Luth.
North Dakota	3	3	
South Dakota	6	6	
Nebraska	12	11	1 R. C. (professional dept. open)
Kansas	19	17	2 R. C.
Montana	3	3	
Wyoming	1	1	
Colorado	4	3	1 R. C.
Arizona	1	1	
Utah	2	2	
Nevada	1	1	
Idaho	1	1	
Washington	9	7	2 R. C.
Oregon	8	8	
California	12	9	3 R. C.
Indian Territory	2	2	
Oklahoma	1	1	
Total	217	182	22 R. C., 6 Luth., 1 Ger. Ev., 1 Dutch Ref., 1 P. E., 1 Cong.

II. *14 southern and 2 southern middle states*			
STATES	Total no. cols.	Coed.	Men only
Delaware	2	1	Delaware college. (The one coeducational college is for negroes.)
Maryland	11	4	4 R. C., St. John's, Maryland agric. college, Johns Hopkins.
District of Columbia	6	3	3 R. C.
Virginia	10	4	2 M. E. So., Univ. of Virginia, Hampden-Sidney, Washington and Lee, William and Mary.
West Virginia	3	3	
North Carolina	15	10	1 R. C., 2 Presb., 1 Luth., 1 Bapt.
South Carolina	9	7	1 A. M. E., College of Charleston.
Georgia	11	6	2 Bapt., 1 A. M. E., 1 M. E. So., Univ. of Georgia,
Florida	6	5	1 R. C.
Kentucky	13	9	1 R. C., 1 Bapt., 1 Presb., Ogden college.
Tennessee	24	20	1 R. C., 2 Presb., 1 P. E. (Univ. of South.)
Alabama	9	7	2 R. C.
Mississippi	4	2	1 Bapt., 1 M. E. So.
Louisiana	9	3	2 R. C., 1 M. E. So., 1 Cong., Louisiana State univ., Tulane.
Texas	16	12	3 R. C., 1 Presb.
Arkansas	8	8	
Missouri	26	21	3 R. C., 1 Bapt., 1 Presb.
Total	182	125	21 R. C., 5 M. E. So., 6 Bapt., 7 Presb., 1 Luth., 2 A. M. E., 1 P. E., 1 Cong.

III. *6 New England and 3 northern middle states*			
STATES	Total no. cols.	Coed.	Men only
Maine	4	2	1 Bapt. (Colby, limited coed.), Bowdoin
New Hampshire	2		1 R. C., 1 Cong. (Dartmouth)
Vermont	3	2	Norwich university
Massachusetts	9	2	2 R. C., 2 Cong. (Amherst), Harvard, Williams, Clark
Rhode Island	1		Brown
Connecticut	3	1	1 P. E. (Trinity), Yale
New York	23	5	8 R. C., 2 P. E. (Hobart), 1 Bapt. (Colgate), Polytechnic institute of Brooklyn, Hamilton, College of City of New York (boys' high school), Columbia, Union, Rochester, New York university
New Jersey	4		2 R. C., 1 Dutch Ref. (Rutgers), Princeton
Pennsylvania	32	17	4 R. C, 1 Luth., 1 Moravian, 1 Friends (Haverford), 1 Dutch Ref. (Franklin & Marshall), Pennsylvania military college, Philadelphia central high school (boys' high school), Lehigh university, University of Pennsylvania, 3 Presb. (Lafayette, Washington & Jefferson, Lincoln)
Total	81	29	17 R. C., 1 Luth., 3 P. E., 3 Cong., 3 Presb., 2 Bapt., 1 Friends, 2 Dutch Ref., 1 Moravian (The Univ. of Penna. admits women to many departments, but not to full undergraduate work leading to the bachelor's degree)

In the western states it will be observed there are, excluding Roman Catholic colleges and seminaries, out of 195 colleges 182 coeducational and only 13 colleges for men only. All of these except 3 are denominational; 6 belong to the Lutheran, 1 to the Dutch Reformed, 1 to the German Evangelical, 1 to the Episcopalian, and 1 to the Congregationalist. The other 3 are, as we might expect, in the most eastern and the earliest settled of the western states; one in Ohio, Western reserve, which teaches women in a separate women's college; one in Indiana, Wabash college, one of the three most important colleges in Indiana; and one in Illinois, Illinois college. Roman Catholic institutions apart, in 14 states and all 3 territories every college for men is open to women (the one university of the territory of New Mexico, not included in the U. S. education report, is open to women). In the southern states and southern middle states there are, excluding Roman Catholic colleges and seminaries, out of 161, 125 coeducational and only 36 colleges for men only. Among these 36, however, are the most important educational institution in Maryland, the Johns Hopkins university; the most important in Georgia, the University of Georgia; in Louisiana the two most important, the Louisiana state university and Tulane university, and in Virginia the very important University of Virginia.[8] Roman Catholic institutions apart, all the colleges in the states of Alabama, Arkansas, Florida and West Virginia are coeducational. In New England and the northern middle states out of 64 colleges, excluding Roman Catholic colleges and seminaries, only 29, or less than half, are coeducational. The colleges for men only include (with the exception of Cornell) all the largest undergraduate colleges in this section—Harvard, Yale, Columbia, Princeton, Pennsylvania. Maine and Vermont are liberal to women, 2 colleges (3 if we

[8] Two of the three next largest colleges in Virginia—Richmond and Roanoke—admit women, but the advance in women's education in that state has been very recent. Until the establishment of the State normal school in 1883 there was not a scientific laboratory in the state accessible to women; in 1893 the Randolph-Macon Woman's college opened with several laboratories, see Prof. Celestia Parrish, Proceedings 2d Capon Springs conference for education in the south, 1899, p. 68. I am much indebted to the author of this paper for valuable data in regard to coeducation in the south.

> count the limited coeducational college of Colby) in Maine and 3 in Vermont being coeducational, but the total number of students in college in these states is very small (in Maine only 843 men and 189 women; in Vermont only 301 men and 99 women). The leading colleges of New Hampshire, Rhode Island, Connecticut, New Jersey and Pennsylvania are closed, and in Massachusetts only 2 are open and 7 closed.[9]

Of the four hundred and eighty colleges for men enumerated by the commissioner of education 336, or 70 per cent (or, excluding Catholic colleges, 80 per cent), admit women. It would be misleading, however, to count among American institutions for higher education, properly so-called, most of the coeducational colleges and separate colleges for men included in this list, and it would be equally misleading to compare the number of women studying in such colleges in the United States with the number of women engaged in higher studies in England, France and Germany.[10] In

[9] The Massachusetts institute of technology is classified by the U. S. ed. reps. among technical schools.

[10] The commissioner of education does not feel himself at liberty to discriminate among the colleges chartered by the different states, but it is well known that in most states the name of college, or preferably that of university, and the power to confer degrees are granted to any institution whatsoever without regard to endowment, scientific equipment, scholarly qualifications of the faculty or adequate preparation of the students. The majority of the so-called colleges and universities of the south and west are really secondary schools. In most of them not only are the greater part of the students really pupils in the preparatory or high school department, but most of the students in the collegiate departments are at graduation barely able to enter upon the sophomore or second year work of the best eastern colleges. Throughout this monograph I have used the word college in speaking of institutions for undergraduate education, except when quoting their official titles, and this whether the college in question is, or is not, included in a larger institution providing also three years of graduate instruction. The terms college and university are used in America without any definite understanding, even among colleges and universities themselves, as to how they shall be differentiated. Probably the most commonly accepted usage is to call an institution a university if it has attached to it various departments, or schools, without regard to the standing of these departments, the preparation of the students entering them, or the work done in them. In this sense all the state universities of the west are called universities because, although many of them are really high schools, they have attached to them schools of pharmacy, veterinary science, agriculture, and sometimes medicine or law. It is in this sense that many institutions for negroes are called universities, because they include various departments of industrial art as well as a high school department. Until very recently the requirements for admission to the departments of law, medicine, dentistry, etc., have been so low that it has been a positive disadvantage to have such schools attached to the college department, and when lately the graduates of Harvard college decided not

order to obtain a better idea of opportunities for true collegiate work open to women at the present time in the United States I have selected from these four hundred and eighty colleges and from the numerous colleges for women classified elsewhere, a list of fifty-eight colleges properly so-called, employing for the purpose the four means of classification most likely to commend themselves to the impartial student of such things.[11]

---

to allow the graduates of its affiliated schools to vote with them for representatives on the board of trustees, they claimed with justice that the illiberal education of the majority of these graduates would tend to lower the standard of Harvard college. The use of the word university should be strictly limited to institutions offering at least three years of graduate instruction in one or more schools.

[11] In this list of fifty-eight colleges I have included: first, the twenty-four colleges (indicated in the list by "a") whose graduates are admitted to the Association of collegiate alumnæ; second, the twenty-three colleges (24 are included in the Federation, but Barnard has ceased to be a graduate school, see page 29) included in the Federation of graduate clubs (indicated by "b"); third, the fifty-two colleges (indicated by "c") included in the 1899–1900 edition of Minerva, the well-known handbook of colleges and universities of the world published each year by Truebner & Co.; and fourth, the colleges which, according to the U. S. education report for 1897–98, have at least $500,000 worth of productive funds (indicated by "d"), and also three hundred or more students (indicated by "e"). In the case of state universities the money they receive annually from national and state appropriations may reasonably be regarded as a sort of supplementary endowment; I have, therefore, included the state universities of Maine, Iowa and West Virginia, whose productive funds do not amount to $500,000. This list of fifty-eight colleges, arranged according to the different sections of the country, and as far as possible in the order of the numbers in their undergraduate departments, is as follows: *New England and 3 northern middle states*: Harvard (bcde), Yale (bcde), Cornell (abcde-coed.), Massachusetts institute of technology (acde-coed.), Smith (acde-woman's college), Princeton (bcde), Pennsylvania (bcde), Columbia (bcde), Brown (bcde), Wellesley (abce-woman's college), Vassar (acde-woman's college), Syracuse (acde-coed.), Dartmouth (cde), Boston (acde-coed.), Amherst (cde), Radcliffe (abce-affiliated), Williams (cde), Lehigh (cde), Maine (e-coed.), Wesleyan (acde-coed.), Vermont (c-coed.), Lafayette (c), Bryn Mawr (abed-woman's college), New York University (cd), Barnard (a-affiliated), Hamilton (c), Colgate (cd), Clark (bcd-no undergrad. department). *Southern and 2 southern middle states*: Missouri (bcde-coed.), Texas (cde-coed.), Columbian (bce-coed.), West Virginia (e-coed.), Tulane (cd), Vanderbilt (bcd-coed.), Virginia (c), Johns Hopkins (bcd), Washington (St. Louis) (cd-coed.), Georgetown (c-Catholic), Catholic university (cd-no undergrad. department). *Western states*: Minnesota (abcde-coed.), Michigan (abcde-coed.), California (abcde-coed.), Wisconsin (abcde-coed.), Chicago (abcde-coed.), Leland Stanford (abcde-coed.), Nebraska (ace-coed.), Ohio state university (de-coed.), Indiana (cde-coed.), Illinois (ce-coed.), Kansas (ace-coed.), Ohio Wesleyan (cde-coed.), Iowa (e-coed.), Northwestern (acde-coed.), Oberlin (acde-coed.), Cincinnati (cd-coed.), Colorado (c-coed.), Western reserve (bcd), College for Women of western reserve (a-affiliated).

The only attempt hitherto made in America to discriminate between colleges of

Of these fifty-eight colleges four are independent colleges for women and three women's colleges affiliated to colleges for men; of the remaining 51, 30, or 58.8 per cent, are coeducational, and a nearer examination makes a much more favorable showing for coeducation. Of the 21 colleges closed to women in their undergraduate departments five have affiliated to them a women's college through which women obtain some share in the undergraduate instruction given, the affiliated colleges in three cases being of enough importance to appear in the same list. Of these five, four (all but Harvard) admit women without restriction to their graduate instruction, and in addition Yale, the University of Pennsylvania and New York university make no distinction between men and women in graduate instruction. The Johns Hopkins university maintains a coeducational medical school. In this list then of fifty-eight, which includes all the most important colleges in the United States, there are, apart from the two Catholic colleges, only ten (Dartmouth, Amherst, Williams, Clark, Princeton, Lehigh, Lafayette, Hamilton, Colgate, Virginia, all situated on the Atlantic seaboard) to which women are not admitted in some departments. Princeton is the only one of the large university foundations that excludes women from any share whatsoever in its advantages. The diagram on the opposite page shows the steady progress of coeducation from 1870 to 1898.[12]

true college grade and others has been made by the Association of collegiate alumnæ. This association was organized in 1882 for the purpose of uniting women graduates of the foremost coeducational colleges and colleges for women only into an association for work connected with the higher education of women. In the early years of the association there was appointed a committee on admissions, and the admission of each successive college in the association has been carefully considered, both with regard to its entrance requirements, the training of its faculty and its curriculum. The Association of collegiate alumnæ concerns itself, of course, only with colleges admitting women, but there is no doubt that the fifteen coeducational colleges and seven colleges for women only admitted to the association would, in the estimation of every one familiar with the subject, rank among the first fifty-eight colleges of the United States.

The Federation of graduate clubs is an association of graduate students of those colleges whose graduate schools are important enough to entitle them to admission to the federation. The colleges in the Federation of graduate clubs are the only colleges in the United States that do true university work.

[12] In only two instances, so far as I know, has coeducation once introduced been abandoned or restricted in any way. The private college of Adelbert of Western reserve, coeducational from 1873, opened a separate woman's college and excluded women in 1888. As the college department was very small and the state of Ohio in which the college was situated the most eastern in feeling of all western states, the change was seemingly to be attributed to a bid for students through undergraduate novelty. The Baptist college of Colby, in Maine, coeducational from 1871, has taught women in separate classes in required

GROWTH OF COEDUCATION

I have prepared the diagram for 1870 from the U. S. ed. rep. for 1870, pp. 506–516, and the diagram for 1897–98 from the U. S. ed. rep., pp. 1848–1867, and from the table, opposite page 6 of this monograph. The diagrams for 1880 and 1890 are copied from the report for 1889–90, p. 764. For assistance in the preparation of this and other diagrams, and in working out the percentages given here, and elsewhere, in this monograph I am much indebted to Dr. Isabel Maddison.

If Catholic colleges are excluded, as in the map opposite page v, coeducational colleges formed, in 1898, 80 per cent, and colleges for men only 20 per cent of the whole number—a still more favorable result for coeducation.

work since 1890. Women are not allowed to compete with men for college prizes or for membership in the students' society, which elects its members on account of scholarship. Complete separation, which was at first planned, has proved impracticable and from the beginning of the sophomore year women and men recite together in all elective work.

All the arguments against the coeducation of the sexes in colleges have been met and answered by experience. It was feared at first that coeducation would lower the standard of scholarship on account of the supposed inferior quality of women's minds. The unanimous experience in coeducational colleges goes to show that the average standing of women is slightly higher than the average standing of men.[13] Many reasons for the greater success of women are given, such as absence of the distraction of athletic sports, greater diligence, higher moral standards, but the fact, however it may be explained, remains and is as gratifying as astonishing to those interested in women's education. The question of health has also been finally disposed of; thousands of women have been working side by side with men in coeducational institutions for the past twenty-five years and undergoing exactly the same tests without a larger percentage of withdrawals on account of illness than men. The question of conduct has also been disposed of. None of the difficulties have arisen that were feared from the association of men and women of marriageable age. Looking at coeducation as a whole it is most surprising that it has worked so well.[14] Perhaps the only objection that may be made from men's point of view to coeducation in America is that it has succeeded only too well and that the proportion of women students is increasing too steadily. Not only is the number of coeducational colleges increasing but the number of women relatively to the number of men is increasing also. In 1890 there were studying in coeducational colleges 16,959 men and 7,929 women; or women, in other words, formed 31.9 per cent of the whole body of students. In 1898 there were 28,823 men and 16,284 women studying in coeducational colleges, women forming 36.1 per cent of the whole body of students. Between 1890 and 1898 men in coeducational colleges have increased 70.0 per cent, but women in

[13] In an investigation made several years ago in the University of Wisconsin, which has been open to women since 1874, it was found that the women ranked in scholarship very considerably beyond the men. In the University of Michigan, where women have been educated with men since 1870, President Angell has repeatedly laid stress on their excellent scholarship. When in 1893–94 a committee of the faculty of the University of Virginia asked the officers of a large number of coeducational colleges especially in regard to this point the testimony received was very remarkable. In England it should be noted that the question of the success of women in collegiate studies has been put beyond a doubt by the published class lists of the competitive honor examinations of Oxford and Cambridge. In the discussions in regard to granting women degrees at Cambridge, it was freely admitted that women's minds were "splendid for examination purposes."

[14] For a discussion of coeducation in schools and colleges in 1892, see U. S. education report for 1891–92, pp. 783–862.

coeducational colleges have increased 105.4 per cent.[15]

There is every reason to suppose that this increase of women will continue. Already girls form 56.5 per cent of the pupils in all secondary schools and 13 per cent of the girls enrolled and only 10 per cent of the boys enrolled graduate from the public high schools. It is sometimes said that men students, as a rule, dislike the presence of women, and in especial that they are unwilling to compete for prizes against women for the very reason that the average standing of women is higher than their own. If there is any force in this statement, however, it would seem that men should increase less rapidly in coeducational colleges than in separate colleges for men. The reverse, however, is the case. During the eight years from 1890 to 1898 men have increased in coeducational colleges 70.0 per cent, but in separate colleges for men only 34.7 per cent.[16] This is all the more remarkable, because in the separate colleges for men are included the large undergraduate departments of Harvard, Yale, Princeton, Columbia and the University of Pennsylvania. It is women who have shown a preference for separate education; women have increased more rapidly in separate colleges for women than in coeducational colleges. It will be observed, however, that the separate colleges for women, like the separate colleges for men included in my list of fifty-eight, are in the east; it is in the east only that any preference for separate education is shown by either sex.[17]

[15] U. S. education report 1889–90, pp. 761, 1582–1599, and 1897–98, p. 1823; account is taken of students of true college grade only in the college proper. Throughout this monograph I have corrected the figures of the U. S. ed. reps. which are affected by the erroneous assumption that the undergraduate departments of Brown, Yale, Rochester, New York Univ., Pennsylvania, Tulane and Western Reserve are coeducational. In the University of Chicago women formed, in 1898, 54.5 per cent of all regular, and 70 per cent of all unclassified, students; in Boston university in the regular college course there were, in 1899, 299 women as against 192 men.

[16] In 1889–90 there were 19,245 men studying in 146 colleges for men only; in 1898–99 there were 25,915 men studying in 143 colleges for men only, an increase of only 34.7 per cent. (In enumerating students I have regarded the limited coeducational college of Colby as coeducational.) Women, however, have increased in women's colleges 138.4 per cent.

[17] The objection of men students in the east to coeducation seems to be mainly in the apprehension that the presence of women may interfere with the free social life which has become so prominent a feature of private colleges for men in the east. These colleges are, for the most part, situated either in small country towns, or in the suburbs of a city, in communities which have grown up about the college, and their students live largely in college dormitories; the conditions, therefore, are exceedingly unlike those prevailing in non-residential colleges and also unlike those prevailing in the world at large. These

Independent colleges for women—Since independent colleges for women of the same grade as those for men are peculiar to the United States, I shall treat them somewhat more fully.[18] The independent colleges here taken into account are the eleven colleges included in division A[19] of the U. S. education reports.[20] The independent colleges for women fall

exceptional conditions are a source of pleasure and, in many respects, of advantage to the student. Undoubtedly there is in coeducational colleges less unrestraint; young men undoubtedly care much for the impression that they make on young women of the same age, and there is more decorum and perhaps more diligence in classrooms where women are present. The objection to coeducation on the part of women students is, to some extent, the same; separate colleges for women in like manner are, as a rule, academic communities living according to regulations and customs all their own; women also feel themselves more unrestrained when they are studying in women's colleges. Then, too, coeducation in the east is still regarded as in some measure an experiment, to the success of which the conduct of each individual woman may, or may not, contribute, and the knowledge of this tends to increase the self-consciousness of student life.

[18] In the case of the colleges in groups I and II these statistics have been obtained through the kindness of the presidents of the colleges concerned; they are for the year 1900, except the numbers of instructors and students which are obtained from the catalogues for the year 1898–99; in enumerating the instructors, presidents, teachers of gymnastics, elocution, music and art have been omitted. Instructors away on leave of absence are not counted among instructors for the current year.

[19] Women's colleges were first classified in division A and division B in 1887. In these reports there appeared sporadically in division A Ingham university, at Leroy, New York, and Rutgers female college in New York city. Neither of these had any adequate endowment and neither ever obtained more than 35 students. Ingham university closed in 1893, Rutgers female college in 1895.

[20] The women's colleges, so called, included in division B of these reports, are in reality church and private enterprise schools, as a rule of the most superficial character, without endowment, or fixed curriculum, or any standard whatsoever of scholarship in teachers or pupils. What money there is to spend is for the most part used to provide teachers of music, drawing and other accomplishments, and the school instruction proper is shamefully inadequate. Few if any of these schools are able to teach the subjects required for entrance to a college properly so called; the really good girls' schools are, as a rule, excluded from this list by their honesty in not assuming the name of college. The U. S. education report for 1886–87 gives 152 of these colleges in division B, the report for 1897–98, 135. When it is said that separate colleges for women are decreasing, the statement is based on this list of colleges in division B, which are not really colleges at all; and when it is said that women students are not increasing so rapidly in separate colleges for women as in coeducational colleges, it is the students in these miscalled colleges who are referred to; for precisely the reverse is true of students in genuine colleges for women. It is happily true that since better college education has been obtainable, women have been refusing to attend the institutions included in class B. Between 1890 and 1898 women have increased only 4.9 per cent in the college departments of such institutions, whereas, in these same eight years, they have increased 138.4 per cent in women's colleges in division

readily into three groups: I. The so-called "four great colleges for women," Vassar, Smith, Wellesley, Bryn Mawr. It will be seen by referring to the classification on page 13 that these four colleges are included among the fifty-eight leading colleges of the United States; they are all included in the twenty-two colleges admitted to the Association of collegiate alumnæ; two of them, Bryn Mawr and Wellesley, are included in the twenty-three colleges belonging to the Federation of graduate clubs; they are all included in the list of fifty-two leading colleges of the United States given in the handbook of Minerva; they are all, except Bryn Mawr, included in the list given by the U. S. education report for 1897–98[21] of forty-six colleges in the United States having three hundred students and upward; three of them, Bryn Mawr, Smith and Vassar, are included among the fifty-two colleges of the United States possessing invested funds of $500,000 and upward, and two of them, Vassar and Bryn Mawr, are included among the twenty-nine colleges of the United States possessing funds of $1,000,000 and upward; three of them, Smith, Wellesley and Vassar, rank among the twenty-three largest undergraduate colleges in the United States; one of them, Smith, ranks as the tenth undergraduate college in the United States.

Vassar college, Poughkeepsie, New York[22]—Founder,

A. The value of statistics of women college students is often vitiated by the fact that women studying in institutions included in division B are counted among college students. Many of the colleges for men only and of the coeducational colleges included in the lists of the commissioner of education are very low in grade, but few of them are so scandalously inefficient as the majority of the girls' schools included in division B. I have, therefore, in my statistics taken no account whatever of women studying in institutions classified in division B.

[21] See pp. 1821, 1822, 1888, 1889. Bryn Mawr had not 300 undergraduate students in 1897–98, but the next year, 1898–99, passed the limit. I have excluded Western reserve as it is not coeducational in its undergraduate department, and, in 1899, had only 182 men in its men's college and 183 women in its women's college.

[22] To any one familiar with the circumstances it does not admit of discussion that in Vassar we have the legitimate parent of all future colleges for women which were to be founded in such rapid succession in the next period. It is true that in 1855 the Presbyterian synod opened Elmira college in Elmira, New York, but it had practically no endowment and scarcely any college students. Even before 1855 two famous female seminaries were founded which did much to create a standard for the education of girls. In 1821 Mrs. Emma Willard opened at Troy a seminary for girls, known as the Troy female seminary, still existing under the name of the Emma Willard school. In 1837 Mary Lyon opened in the beautiful valley of the Connecticut Mt. Holyoke seminary, where girls were educated so cheaply that it was almost a free school. This institution has had a great influence in the higher education of women; it became in 1893 Mt. Holyoke college. These seminaries

Matthew Vassar; intention, "to found and equip an institution which should accomplish for young women what our colleges are accomplishing for young men;" opened, 1865; preparatory department dropped, 1888; presidents, three (men); 45 instructors (16 Ph. D.s.)—35 women, 2 without first degree; 10 men; 584 undergrad. s., 11 grad. s., 24 special s.; productive funds, $1,050,000; a main building with lecture rooms, library and accommodation for 345 students, and two other residence halls accommodating 189 students; a science building; a lecture building; a museum with art, music and laboratory rooms; an observatory; a gymnasium; a plant house; a president's house; five professors' houses; total cost of buildings, $1,044,365; vols. in library, 30,000; laboratory equipment, $33,382; acres, 200; music and art depts., but technical work in neither counted toward bachelor's degree; tuition fee, $100; lowest charge, tuition, board and residence, including washing, $400.

Wellesley college, Wellesley, Massachusetts—Founder, Henry F. Durant; intention, "to found a college for the glory of God by the education and culture of women," opened 1875; preparatory department dropped, 1880; requirement from students of one hour daily domestic or clerical work dropped, 1896; presidents, five (all women); 69 instructors (13 Ph. D.s.)—64 women, 16, apart from laboratory assistants without first degree; 5 men; 611 undergrad. s., 25 grad. s., 21 special s.; productive funds, $7,000;[23] a main building with library lecture rooms and accommodation for 250 students; a chemical laboratory; an observatory; a

are often claimed as the first women's colleges, but their curriculum of study proves conclusively that they had no thought whatever of giving women a collegiate education, whereas, the deliberations of the board of trustees whom Mr. Vassar associated with himself show clearly that it was expressly realized that here for the first time was being created a woman's college as distinct from the seminary or academy. In 1861 the movement for the higher education of women had scarcely begun. It was not until eight years later that the first of the women's colleges at Cambridge, England, opened.

[23] The founder of Wellesley expected to leave the college a large endowment, but his fortune was dissipated in unfortunate investments. The splendid grounds and many halls of residence of the college constitute a form of endowment, otherwise its lack of productive funds would have excluded it from class I.

chapel; an art building; a music building; 8 halls of residence, accommodating 348 students (new hall being built); total cost of buildings, $1,106,500; vols, in library, 49,970; laboratory equipment, $50,000; acres, 410; music and art depts., but technical work in neither counted toward bachelor's degree; tuition fee, $175; lowest charge, tuition, board and residence (beds made, rooms dusted by students), $400.

Smith college, Northampton, Massachusetts—Founder, Sophia Smith; intention, to provide "means and facilities for education equal to those which are afforded in our colleges for young men;" opened, 1875; no preparatory department ever connected with the college; president, one (man); 49 instructors (13 Ph. D.s.)—27 women, 9 without first degree; 12 men; 1,070 undergrad. s., 4 grad. s.; since 1891 no special s. admitted; productive funds, $900,000; two lecture buildings; a lecture and gymnastic building; a science building; a chemical laboratory; an observatory; a gymnasium; a plant house; a music building; an art building; 13 halls of residence accommodating 520 students; a president's house; total cost of buildings $786,000; vols, in library, 8,000 (70,000 vols. in library in Northampton also used by the students); laboratory equipment, $22,500; acres, 40; music and art depts., technical work in both, amounting to between one-sixth and one-seventh of the hours required for a degree, may be counted toward bachelor's degree; tuition fee, $100; lowest charge, tuition, board and residence (beds made, rooms dusted by students), $400.

Bryn Mawr college, Bryn Mawr, Pennsylvania—Founder, Joseph W. Taylor; intention, to provide "an institution of learning for the advanced education of women which should afford them all the advantages of a college education which are so freely offered to young men;" opened, 1885; no preparatory department ever connected with the college; presidents, two (one man, one woman); 38 instructors (29 Ph. D.s. 1 D. Sc.)—15 women, 23 men; 269 undergrad, s., 61 grad. s., 9 hearers; productive funds,

$1,000,000; a lecture and library building; a science building; a gymnasium; an infirmary; five halls of residence and two cottages, accommodating 323 students; a president's house; 6 professors' houses; total cost, $718,810; vols. in library, 32,000; laboratory equipment, $47,998; acres, 50; no music department; no technical instruction in art; tuition fee, $125; lowest charge, tuition, board and residence, $400.

II. The women's colleges not included in the list of the fifty-eight most important colleges in the United States given on page 13, but of exceedingly good academic standing as compared with the greater number of the separate colleges for men and the coeducational colleges included in the four hundred and eighty enumerated by the commissioner of education.

Mt. Holyoke college, South Hadley, Massachusetts—Founder, Mary Lyon; seminary opened, 1837; chartered as seminary and college, 1888; seminary department dropped and true college organized, 1893; presidents, two (both women); 37 instructors (7 Ph. D.s.)—all women; 5, apart from laboratory assistants, without first degree; 426 undergrad, s., 3 grad. s., 9 special s., 3 music s.; productive funds, $300,000; a lecture building; a science building; a museum and art gallery; a library; a gymnasium; a rink; an observatory; an infirmary; a plant house; 9 residence halls accommodating 478 students; total cost of buildings, $625,000; vols. in library, 17,700; laboratory equipment, $33,000; acres, 160; music and art depts., technical work in both, amount limited by faculty, may be counted towards bachelor's degree; tuition fee, $100; lowest charge, tuition, board and residence (beds made, rooms dusted, by students, and in addition one-half hour of domestic work required), $250.

Woman's college of Baltimore, city of Baltimore, Maryland—Founded and controlled by Methodist Episcopal church; opened, 1888; preparatory department dropped, 1893; presidents, two (men); 21 instructors (10 Ph. D.s.)—11 women, 1 without first degree; 10 men, 1 without first degree; 259 undergrad. s.; 0 grad. s.; 15 special s.; productive funds, $334,994; a lecture building and three houses adapted for lecture purposes; a gymnasium; a biological laboratory; 3 residence halls holding 230; total cost of buildings, $505,703; vols. in library, 7,800; laboratory equipment, $47,000; acres (in city), 7; music and art depts., but technical work in neither counted towards bachelor's degree; tuition fee, $125; lowest charge, tuition, board and residence (beds made, rooms dusted by students), $375.

Wells college, Aurora, New York—Founders, Henry Wells and Edwin B. Morgan; seminary opened, 1868; chartered as college, 1870; preparatory dept. dropped, 1896; presidents, two (men); 13 instructors (4 Ph. D.s.)—10 women, 3 without first degree; 3 men; 59 undergrad. s.; 0 grad. s.; 27 special s.; 4 music s.; productive funds, $200,000; a main building with lecture rooms and accommodations for 100 students; a science and music building; a president's house; total cost of buildings, $195,000; vols. in library, 7,300; laboratory equipment, $20,200; acres, 200; music and art depts., technical work in neither counted towards bachelor's degree; tuition fee, $100; lowest charge, tuition, board and residence (beds made by students), $400.

III. Elmira college, the Randolph-Macon Woman's college, Rockford college and Mills college are here relegated to a third group because of certain common characteristics. Their endowment is wholly inadequate, averaging considerably less than $50,000 apiece, reaching $100,000 only in the case of the Randolph-Macon Woman's college. In each of them a disproportionate number of students is studying in the music or art department; special students form too large a proportion of the whole number of students; the number of professors is too small to permit college classes to be conducted by specialists; the college classes are too small; true college training cannot be obtained in very small classes, and moreover, in view of the increasing number of women now going to college, when a college for women does not grow steadily it is reasonable to assume that there must be some good reason for its lack of growth.

Elmira college, situated at Elmira, New York, has, apart from the president, 10 academic instructors (7 women, 2 without first degree; 3 men); 5 teachers of music, 2 of art. There are studying in the college 70 regular college students, 17 specials and 61 special students in music.

The Randolph-Macon Woman's college, situated at Lynchburg, Virginia, has, apart from the president, 12 academic instructors (2 Ph. D.s.)—7 women, 2 without first degree; 5 men; 9 instructors in music. Of the 226 students,[24] 55 are regular college students; 44 registered for degree but spending one-fifth of time in music or preparatory work; 16 special students; 6 students of art; 49 preparatory students; 46 students of music.

Rockford college, Rockford, Illinois—Opened as seminary, 1849; chartered as college, 1892; 13 academic instructors (2 Ph. D.s.)—all women, 3 without first degree; 4 teachers of music, 1 of art; 35 college s.; 7 special s.; 70 s. in music only.

Mills college, California—Opened as seminary, 1871; chartered as college, 1885; 11 instructors (9 women, 3 without first degree; 2 men); 8 teachers of music; 22 college s.; 135 pupils in preparatory department.

In addition to the existing colleges belonging to these groups, a separate college for women, Trinity, meant to be of true college grade, will soon be opened in Washington under the control of the Roman Catholic church.

It is often assumed by the adversaries of coeducation that independent colleges for women may be trusted to introduce a course of study modified especially for women, but the experience, both of coeducational colleges that have devised women's courses and of women's colleges, demonstrates conclusively that women themselves refuse to regard as satisfactory any modification whatsoever of the usual academic course. At the opening of Vassar college itself it is clear that the trustees and faculty made an honest

[24] The numbers of students are for the year 1899–1900.

attempt to discover and introduce certain modifications in the system of intellectual training then in operation in the best colleges for men. They planned from the start to give much more time to accomplishments—music, drawing and painting—than was given in men's colleges, and the example of Vassar in this respect was followed ten years later by Wellesley and Smith. These accomplishments have gradually fallen out of the course of women's colleges; neither Vassar nor Wellesley allows time spent in them to be counted toward the bachelor's degree. Smith alone of the colleges of group I still permits nearly one-sixth of the whole college course to be devoted to them. Bryn Mawr, which opened ten years later than Smith or Wellesley, from the beginning found it possible to exclude them from its course.

In like manner Vassar, Smith and Wellesley in the beginning found it necessary to admit special students—students, that is to say, interested in special subjects, but without sufficient general training to be able to matriculate as college students; but their admission has been recognized as disadvantageous, and has gradually been restricted. In 1870 special students, as distinguished from preparatory students, formed 19.6 per cent of the whole number of the students of Vassar; in 1899 they formed only 3.9 per cent, and only 3.3 per cent of the whole number of Wellesley students. Smith since 1891 has declined to admit them at all, and Bryn Mawr never admitted them.[25]

Again, Wellesley and Vassar in the beginning organized preparatory departments with pupils living in the same halls as the college students and taught in great part by the same teachers. The presence of these pupils tended to turn the colleges into boarding schools, and the steady and rapid development of Vassar as a true college began only after the closing of its preparatory department in 1888; until this time the number of students in the college proper had been almost stationary; Wellesley closed its preparatory department in 1880; Smith never organized one; Bryn Mawr never organized one; Mt. Holyoke, the Woman's college of Baltimore, and Wells college have all closed their preparatory departments within the last

[25] To the women's colleges of group III they are admitted still in large numbers, and they still form 35.1 per cent of all the undergraduate students in the affiliated college of Radcliffe, and 35.7 per cent of all the undergraduate students in the affiliated college of Barnard; in part, perhaps, because these colleges are largely dependent upon their tuition fees, and in part too, no doubt, because the presence of special students is less

seven years.[26]

It seems to have been at first supposed that the same standards of scholarship need not be applied in the choice of instructors to teach women as in that of instructors to teach men, that women were fittest to teach women, and that the personal character and influence of the woman instructor in some mysterious way supplied the deficiency on her part of academic training. For a long time not even an ordinary undergraduate education was required of her, and there are still teaching in women's colleges too many women without even a first degree. But it has been found on the whole that systematic mental training is best imparted by those who have themselves received it; the numbers of well-trained women are increasing; and the

---

disadvantageous where there is no dormitory life.

[26] Colleges for women draw their students from private schools to a much greater extent than do coeducational colleges; and it was the very great inefficiency of these schools that induced the earlier colleges for women to organize preparatory departments of their own. The entrance examinations of the women's colleges are the only influence for good that has ever been brought to bear upon the feeble teaching of these schools. In 1874, before the numbers of women wishing to prepare for college were great enough to influence the private schools, a plan for raising their standard was devised by the Woman's education association of Boston, at whose request Harvard university for 7 years conducted a series of examinations modeled on the Oxford and Cambridge higher local examinations which have been such an efficient agency in England. Committees of women were organized in different cities, and an attempt was made to induce girls' schools to send up candidates for these examinations. In 7 years, however, only 106 candidates offered themselves for the preliminary examination, and only 36 received a complete certificate. In 1881 the entrance examinations of Harvard college were substituted for these special women's examinations, in the hope that the interest in reaching the standard set by Harvard for its entering class of men might add to the number of candidates; but even after this change was made comparatively few candidates took the examinations, and in 1896 the effort was discontinued; the Harvard examinations have been used from that time onward simply as the ordinary entrance examinations of Radcliffe college. In Great Britain the Cambridge higher local examinations are taken annually by about 900 women. There was needed some such pressure as is brought to bear by pupils determined to go to college to induce private schools to add college graduates to their staff of teachers. The requirements for admission to Bryn Mawr college have to my personal knowledge been a most important factor in introducing college-bred women as teachers into all the more important private girls' schools of Philadelphia and in many private schools elsewhere; and every college for women drawing students from private schools has the same experience. On the other hand, every relaxation in the requirements for admission, such as the practice of admitting on certificate adopted by Vassar, Wellesley and Smith, tends to deprive girls' schools of a much needed stimulus. Radcliffe and Barnard, like Bryn Mawr, insist upon examination for admission and decline to accept certificates.

prejudice against the appointment of men where men are better qualified has almost disappeared.[27]

It has been recognized that the work done in women's colleges is most satisfactory to women when it is the same in quality and quantity as the work done in colleges for men, and it has been recognized also that they need the same time for its performance. Domestic work, therefore, which by the founder of Wellesley was regarded as a necessary part of women's education, is at present, I believe, required nowhere except on the perfectly plain ground of economy. The hour of domestic service originally required of every student in Wellesley was abandoned in 1896; a half-hour is still required at Mt. Holyoke, but tuition, board and residence are less expensive there. The time given to domestic work is obviously so much time taken from academic work.

In the matter of discipline the tendency has been toward ever-diminishing supervision by the college authorities. Vassar and Wellesley began with the strict regulations of a boarding school; it was regarded as impossible that young women living away from home should be in any measure trusted with the control of their own actions. Smith from the first allowed more liberty, in part because many of her students lived in boarding houses outside the college. In all three colleges the restrictions laid upon the students have been gradually lessened, and at Vassar there is at present a well-developed system of what is known as "limited self-government," according to which many matters of discipline are intrusted to the whole body of students. Bryn Mawr was organized with a system of self-government by the students perhaps more far-reaching than was then in operation in any of the colleges for men; the necessary rules are made by the Students' association, which includes all undergraduate and graduate students, and enforced by an executive committee of students who in the case of a serious offense may recommend the suspension or expulsion of the offender, and whose recommendation,

[27] Until Bryn Mawr opened in 1885 with a large staff of young unmarried men, it had been regarded as almost out of the question to appoint unmarried men in a women's college; now they are teaching in all colleges for women. The same instructors pass from colleges for men to colleges for women and from colleges for women to colleges for men, employing in each the same methods of instruction. Some years since one of the professors at Smith college received at the same time offers of a post at the Johns Hopkins, at Columbia, and at Bryn Mawr; and among the professors the most successful in their teaching at Princeton, Chicago and Columbia are men whose whole experience had been gained in teaching women at Bryn Mawr.

when sustained by the whole association, is always accepted by the college. The perfect success of the system has shown that there is no risk in relying to the fullest extent on the discretion of a body of women students.

> **Affiliated colleges**[28]—There are five[29] affiliated colleges in the United States—Radcliffe college, Barnard college, the Women's college of Brown university, the College for Women of Western reserve university, and the H. Sophie Newcomb memorial college for women of Tulane university.[30] The affiliated college in America is modeled on the English women's colleges of Oxford and Cambridge, with such modifications as are made necessary by the wholly different constitution of English and American universities. These modifications, however, it must in fairness be explained, are so essential as to make of it a wholly different institution.[31]

[28] The following data have been furnished me by the courtesy of the presidents or deans of the colleges concerned, except the data of the H. Sophie Newcomb memorial college, for which I am indebted to Professor Evelyn Ordway. These data are for the year 1900; the numbers of instructors and students have been obtained from the catalogues for 1898–99.

[29] In one instance only—that of Evelyn college in New Jersey—has an affiliated college, once established, been compelled to close its doors. Evelyn, however, partook of the nature of a private enterprise school, and was begun on an unacademic basis in 1887. A certain number of Princeton professors consented to serve on the board of trustees and give instruction there, but it was, in reality, a young ladies' finishing school with a few students (in 1891, 22; in 1894, 18; in 1897, 14) pursuing collegiate courses. Music and accomplishments were made much of, and in 1897 the college came to a well-merited end.

[30] Radcliffe and Barnard are the only two of the affiliated colleges that appear in the U. S. education reports in division A of women's colleges. The students of the other three are reported under Brown, Western reserve and Tulane respectively, thus giving these colleges a false air of being coeducational in their undergraduate departments. The endowment and equipment of these three affiliated colleges, although entirely independent of the colleges to which they are affiliated, are given nowhere separately.

[31] It is difficult for those interested in women's education in England to understand the existence in America of independent colleges for women, and if American education were organized like English education they would, indeed, have no reason to exist. In an English university, consisting, as it does, of many separate colleges whose students live in their separate halls of residence, are taught by their own teachers, hear in common with the students of other colleges the lectures offered by the central university organization, and compete against each other in honor examinations conducted by a common board of university examiners, the colleges for women—at Cambridge, Girton and Newnham, and at Oxford, Somerville hall, Lady Margaret hall and St. Hugh's hall—are organized in

Radcliffe college, Cambridge, Massachusetts[32]—Affiliated to Harvard university, union dissoluble after due notice; opened by the Society for the collegiate instruction of women in 1879; incorporated as Radcliffe college with power to confer degrees in 1894; board of trustees and financial management separate from Harvard; B. A. and M. A. degrees conferred by Radcliffe; Ph. D. degree as yet conferred neither by Radcliffe nor Harvard; degrees, instructors, and academic board of control, subject to approval of Harvard; no instructors not instructors at Harvard also; undergraduate instruction at Harvard repeated at Radcliffe at discretion of

---

precisely the same way as colleges for men. They may, or may not, be as well equipped as the best men's colleges, but the difference is a matter of endowment, not of university organization; there are differences also between the various colleges for men. Examinations, again, play a far more important part in English than in American education. There are in Great Britain only a few examining and degree-giving bodies, for whose examinations all the various colleges prepare their students. The degrees mean that certain examinations have been passed, and have a definite and universally acknowledged value. A degree given by an American college means that the person receiving it has lived for some time in a community of a certain kind, enjoying certain opportunities of which he has conscientiously availed himself. For this reason no one of the 491 colleges of the United States enumerated in the U. S. education report for 1897–98 bestows its degree in recognition of examinations passed in any other college. For this reason Harvard college has had logic on its side in declining to confer upon the students completing their undergraduate course in Radcliffe college the Harvard B. A. They have not lived in the same community, nor yet had all the opportunities of the Harvard student. The certificate received by the student of Girton or Newnham represents exactly the same thing as the Cambridge degree; the B. A. of Radcliffe does not represent the same thing as the Harvard B. A. What is represented by the degrees of different colleges in the United States may, or may not, be equal, but never is the same. Nevertheless Columbia, Brown, Tulane and Western reserve confer their degrees upon the women graduates of their affiliated colleges for women.

[32] The first American affiliated college was the so-called Harvard annex, which was brought into existence by the devoted efforts of a small number of influential professors of Harvard college, who voluntarily formed themselves into a "Society for the collegiate instruction of women," and repeated each week to classes of women the lectures and class work they gave to men in Harvard college. The idea first occurred to Mr. Arthur Gilman in 1878. Girton college, Cambridge, England, after which the annex was modeled, had then been in successful operation for nine years. Mrs. Louis Agassiz, the widow of the famous naturalist, agreed to become the official head of the undertaking, and she associated with herself other influential Boston and Cambridge women. Mr. Arthur Gilman became the secretary of the society. The president of Harvard college declared that, so far as the university was concerned, the professors were free to teach women in their leisure hours if they chose. The annex was opened for students in 1879 in a rented house near the Harvard campus with 25 students.

instructors; since 1893 women admitted to graduate and semi-graduate courses given in Harvard, at discretion of instructor, subject to approval of the Harvard faculty; in 1899, 64 such courses open to Radcliffe students; 238 undergrad. s.; 54 grad. s.; 129 special s.; productive funds about $430,000; a lecture and library building; a gymnasium; 4 temporary buildings used for lectures and laboratories; a students' club house; no residence hall, but one about to be built; total cost of buildings about $110,000; vols. in library, 14,138; access to Harvard library and collections; scientific laboratories of Harvard not available; cost of laboratory equipment not ascertainable, inadequate; acres (in city) about 3; tuition fee, $200.

Barnard college, New York city—Affiliated to Columbia university, union dissoluble by either party after year's notice; opened in 1889; status very much that of Radcliffe until January, 1900, when women graduates were admitted without restriction to the graduate school of Columbia, registering in Columbia, not as heretofore in Barnard, and Barnard was incorporated as an undergraduate women's college of the university, its dean voting in the university council, and the president of Columbia becoming its president and a member of its board of trustees; Barnard's faculty consists of the president of the university, the dean of Barnard, and instructors, either men or women, nominated by the dean, approved by Barnard trustees and president of Columbia and appointed by Columbia; courses for A. B. degree and all examinations determined and conducted by Barnard faculty, subject to provisions of university council for maintaining integrity of degree; all degrees conferred by Columbia; after July 1, 1904, no undergraduate courses in Columbia, except in the Teachers' college, will be open to Barnard seniors as heretofore, complete undergraduate work will be given separately at Barnard, not necessarily by same instructors; 131 undergrad. s.; 76 grad. s.; 73 special s.; productive funds, $150,000; one large building containing lecture rooms, laboratories and accommodation for 65 students, cost, $525,000; vols. in reading room, 1,000; access to Columbia, library; scientific laboratories of Columbia not available; cost of laboratory equipment $9,250; land (in city), 200 × 160 feet; tuition fee, $150.

Women's college of Brown university, Providence, Rhode Island—Affiliated to Brown university; university degrees and examinations opened to women, and their undergraduate instruction informally begun in 1892; women's college established by Brown university as a regular department of the university in 1897 under control of the university trustees; advisory council of five women appointed by trustees to advise with president of university and dean of women's college; funds of the women's college held and administered separately by trustees; all degrees conferred by Brown; women and men examined together; required courses given in Brown repeated to women by same instructors; all instruction given by Brown instructors; all graduate work in Brown open to graduate women without restriction since 1892; women recite with men in many of the smaller elective undergraduate courses; 140 undergrad. s.; 38 grad. s.; 25 special s.; a lecture hall costing $38,000; no residence hall; access to Brown library; scientific laboratories of Brown not available; very inadequate laboratory equipment; no productive funds; tuition fee, $105.

College for women of Western reserve university, Cleveland, Ohio—Affiliated to Western reserve university; established by Western reserve in 1888; degrees conferred by Western reserve; graduate department of Western reserve open to graduate women without restriction; separate financial management; separate faculty 21 (9 Ph. D.s.)—14 men, 7 women; 165 undergrad. s.; 18 special s.; productive funds, about $250,000; a lecture hall, a residence hall accommodating 40 students; total cost of buildings, including land, about $200,000; 3 laboratories of men's college available at certain times; access to Western reserve library; tuition, $85; lowest charge, board, room rent and tuition (beds made by students), $335.

H. Sophie Newcomb memorial college for women, New Orleans, Louisiana—Affiliated with Tulane university, but situated in another part of the city; founder, Mrs. Josephine Louise Newcomb; opened 1886; under control of board of trustees of Tulane; graduate department of Tulane university open to graduate women without restriction since 1890; separate financial management; separate president and faculty; 8 instructors (1 Ph. D.)—5 women, 2 without first degrees; 3 men, 1 without first degree; 51 undergrad. s.; 34 special s. (10 in gymnastics); 54 s. of art; 80 pupils in preparatory dept.; art dept.; productive funds, $400,000; a lecture building, a chapel, an art building, a pottery building, two residence halls accommodating 75 students, a high school building; total cost of buildings about $225,000; vols. in library about 6,000; tuition, $100; lowest charge, board, room rent (two in one room, beds made by students) and tuition, $280.

In the smaller group, which includes the College for women of Western reserve university and the H. Sophie Newcomb memorial college, the affiliated college tends to become an entirely separate institution; in its instructors and instruction it differs widely from the institution to which it is affiliated; it is, in fact, a different college called into existence by the same authorities. In the larger group, which includes the Women's college of Brown, Barnard and Radcliffe, the affiliated college tends to blend itself with the institution to which it is affiliated in a new coeducational institution. The ideal in view is a complete identity of instructors and instruction and the law of economy of force forbids attaining this ideal by the duplication of the whole instruction given. It is less wasteful to double the number of hearers in any lecture room than to repeat the lecture. It is in the Women's college of Brown that we find the closest affiliation and, accordingly, the nearest approach to coeducation. The corporation of Brown furnished the land on which Pembroke hall, the academic building of the Women's college, was erected, and accepted the gift of the building when it was completed; Brown has from first to last openly assumed responsibility for its affiliated college in fact as well as name. In the graduate department of

Brown there is, as has been said, unrestricted coeducation; and in many of the smaller undergraduate elective courses women are reciting with men. In the graduate department of Columbia there is now unrestricted coeducation. It is in the case of Radcliffe that there is least approach to coeducation. What has made possible the policy pursued at Radcliffe has been the self-sacrificing zeal of many eminent Harvard professors, willing at any cost of inconvenience to give to women what could seemingly on no other terms be given; but the sacrifice is too great, and in the modern world too unnecessary; it is at present almost everywhere possible for the professor interested in educating women to lighten his own labors by admitting them to the same classes with men. Only the affiliated colleges of the second group present in their internal organization a type essentially different from that of the independent college—a type intermediate between the independent and the coeducational.

Professional Education

Graduate instruction in the faculty of philosophy—True university instruction begins after the completion of the college course, and very little such instruction is given by any American university[33] except in the so-called graduate schools belonging to the twenty-three colleges in the United States included in the Federation of graduate clubs.[34] In the following 16 of these 23 graduate schools women are admitted without restriction and compete with men for many of the scholarships and honors: Yale, Brown, Cornell, Columbia, New York university, Pennsylvania, Columbian,

[33] The medical school of the Johns Hopkins university is a true university school, admitting only holders of the bachelor's degree; the law school of Harvard university is practically a university school, although seniors in Harvard college are received as students.

[34] Out of the 58 most important American colleges enumerated on page 13 only 23, it will be remembered, appear in the lists of the Federation of graduate clubs. Unfortunately it must not be inferred that all these 23 colleges are doing true professional work and offering graduate students a three years' course leading to the degree of Ph. D. In some of them there are provided only courses leading to the degree of A. M., which, like the degree of A. B., indicating general culture. The affiliated college of Radcliffe appears in the list of graduate clubs, although it can scarcely be said to exist independently as a separate graduate school, being virtually the portal by which women are admitted to a limited amount of graduate work at Harvard. In 1899–1900 only 12 graduate lecture courses and 3 research courses were repeated at Radcliffe.

Vanderbilt, Missouri, Western reserve, Chicago, Michigan, Wisconsin, Minnesota, California, Leland Stanford Junior; Bryn Mawr and Wellesley admit women only; Harvard admits them to certain courses through the mediation of Radcliffe. There remain, apart from the Catholic university, only 3 graduate schools excluding women: Clark, Princeton and the Johns Hopkins university; and in the Johns Hopkins they are admitted to at least one university department—that of the medical school.[35]

In 1898–99 there were studying in these 23 graduate schools 1,021 women, forming 26.8 per cent of the whole number of graduate students.[36] In 1889–90 the U. S. education report estimates that there were 271 women graduate students out of a total of 2,041 graduate students, or women formed 13.27 per cent of all graduate students; in 1897–98 the report for that year estimates that there were 1,398 women out of a total of 5,816 graduate students, or women formed 24.04 per cent of all students—a remarkable increase as compared to the increase of men graduate students in 8 years.

[35] The graduate courses of Clark (which has no undergraduate department) are few in number and attended by only 48 men; the exclusion of women is, therefore, very surprising especially as the principal subjects of instruction, pedagogy, experimental psychology and the like, are of peculiar interest to women. The exclusion of women from all but the medical department of the Johns Hopkins university is really of serious import, because the Johns Hopkins university, judged not by numbers but by scholarly research and publication, the number of Ph. D. degrees conferred, and the important college and university positions filled by its graduates, has long been, and perhaps is still, the most important graduate school in the United States. Its attitude toward women is to be accounted for in part by its location, and in part by the fact that its management is in the hands of a self-perpetuating board of twelve trustees appointed originally by the founder, and without exception Baltimoreans, so that no pressure can be brought to bear upon the corporation from more progressive sections of the country.

[36] These figures are taken from the Graduate handbook for 1899, published by the Federation of graduate clubs. Of these the greatest number studying in any one institution in the west was to be found in the University of Chicago, and the next greatest in the University of California; the greatest number studying in any one institution in the east was to be found at Barnard-Columbia, and the next greatest at Bryn Mawr. There were studying in the graduate departments of the University of Chicago (including summer students) 276 women; in the University of California, 90; in Barnard-Columbia, 82; in Bryn Mawr, 61; in Radcliffe-Harvard, 58; in Yale, 42; in Cornell, 36; in the University of Pennsylvania, 34. The position of Bryn Mawr in this series seems to show conclusively that an independent woman's college maintaining a sufficiently high standard of instruction may compete successfully for students with much larger and older coeducational foundations.

Comparative table of the progress of coeducation and increase of women students from 1890 to 1898 and 1899 in theology, law, medicine, dentistry, pharmacy, schools of technology and agriculture.

	1890[37]			1899[38]			1890[39]		1898[40]	
	Number of colleges for men only	Number of coed. colleges	Percentage of coed. colleges	Number of colleges for men only	Number of coed. colleges	Percentage of coed. colleges	Number of women students	Percentage women of all students	Number of women students	Percentage women of all students
Theology	No women reported			97	68	41.2	No women reported		198	2.4
Law	No women reported			22	64	74.4	No women reported		147	1.3

[37] The numbers of coeducational and other professional schools are estimated from the U. S. ed. rep. for 1889–90.

[38] Through the kindness of Mr. James Russell Parsons, Jr., author of the monograph on professional education in the United States, published as one of this series, I am able to insert the figures for 1899, see p. 23. By personal inquiry I have been able to add four to his list of coeducational schools of theology.

[39] The numbers of coeducational and other professional schools are estimated from the U. S. ed. rep. for 1889–90.

[40] The number of professional students for the year 1898 is taken from the U. S. ed. rep. for 1897–98.

Medicine (regular and irregular)[41]	67	46	40.7	69	80	53.7	854	5.5	1397	6.0
Dentistry	14	13	48.1	12	44	78.6	53	2.0	62	2.4
Pharmacy	13	16	55.2	4	48	92.3	60	2.1	174	4.7
Schools of technology and agriculture endowed with national land grant[42]	14	12	46.2	16	48	75.	774	12.5	2281	16.1

[41] For the sake of clearness I have omitted from the above table the 7 separate medical schools for women, although I have counted their students in the total number of women medical students, both in 1890 and 1898. In 1890 there were studying in the 6 regular medical women's colleges 425 women, as against 648 women in coeducational regular medical colleges; in 1898 there were studying in them 411 women, as against 1045 in coeducational colleges, a decrease of 3.3 per cent, whereas women students in coeducational medical colleges have increased 16.3 per cent. I limit the comparison to regular medical schools because women have increased relatively more rapidly in irregular medical schools and there is only one separate irregular medical school for women. It is sometimes said that women prefer medical sects because the proportion of women studying in irregular schools is relatively greater than the proportion studying in regular schools; but in 1898, 85.7 per cent of the irregular schools were coeducational and only 46.6 per cent of regular schools, a fact which undoubtedly increases the proportion of students studying in irregular schools.

[42] The statistics for the schools of technology and agriculture are taken from the U. S. education report for 1889–90, pp. 1053–1054, and from the report for 1897–98, pp. 1985–1988. I have excluded schools of technology not endowed with the national land grant. In 1890 there were 27 of such schools (5 of them coeducational); in 1898 their number had fallen to 17 (3 of them coeducational). Very few women are studying in these schools; in 1898 women formed only 0.2 per cent of all students studying in them.

Graduate fellowships and scholarships—In 1899 there were open to women 319 scholarships varying in value from $100 to $400 (50 of these exclusively for women) and 2 foreign scholarships (1 exclusively for women); 81 residence fellowships of the value of $400 or over (18 of these exclusively for women); 24 foreign fellowships of the value of $500 and upwards (12 of these exclusively for women).[43]

Theology, law, medicine, dentistry, pharmacy, veterinary science, schools of technology and agriculture—Ten years ago there were very few women studying in any of these schools. The wonderful increase both in facilities for professional study and in the number of women students during the last eight years may be seen by referring to the comparative table on page 34-35.

It is evident to the impartial observer that coeducation is to be the method in professional schools. Except in medicine, where women were at first excluded from coeducational study by the strongest prejudice that has ever been conquered in any movement, no important separate professional schools, indeed none whatever, except one unimportant school of pharmacy have been founded for women only.[44] It is evident also that the number of women entering upon professional study is increasing rapidly. If we compare the relative increase of men and of women from 1890 to 1898 we obtain the following percentages: increase of students in medicine, men, 51.1 per cent, women, 64.2 per cent; in dentistry, men, 150.2 per cent, women, 205.7 per cent; in pharmacy, men, 25.9 per cent, women, 190 per cent; in technology and agriculture, men, 119.3 per cent, women, 194.7 per cent.

GENERAL CONSIDERATIONS

There are many questions connected with the college education of American women which possess great interest for the student of social

[43] See Fellowships and graduate scholarships, published by the Association of collegiate alumnæ, Richmond Hill, N. Y., III Series, No. 2, July, 1899.

[44] A private law school for women existed for some years in the city of New York, founded by Madame Kempin, a graduate of the University of Zurich. At the request of the Women's legal education society it was incorporated with the New York University law school.

science.

Number of college women—In the year 1897–98[45] there were studying in the undergraduate and graduate departments of coeducational colleges and universities 17,338 women, and in the undergraduate and graduate departments of independent and affiliated women's colleges, division A, 4,959 women, women forming thus 27.4 per cent of the total number of graduate and undergraduate students. The 22 colleges belonging to the Association of collegiate alumnæ, which are, on the whole, the most important colleges in the United States admitting women, have conferred the bachelor's degree on 12,804 women. If we add to these the graduates of the Women's college of Brown university, 102 in number, and the graduates of the 14 additional coeducational colleges included in my list of the 58 most important colleges in the United States, we obtain, including those graduating in June, 1899, a total of 14,824 women holding the bachelor's degree.[46] There is thus formed, even leaving out of account the graduates of the minor colleges, a larger body of educated women than is to be found in any other country in the world. These graduates have received the most strenuous college training obtainable by women in the United States, which does not differ materially from the best college training obtainable by American men (indeed, women graduates of coeducational colleges have received precisely the same training as men), and may fairly be compared with the women who have received college and university training abroad. In other countries women university graduates, or even women who have

[45] See U. S. ed. rep. 1897–98, p. 1825, corrected according to note 16, page 16 of this monograph.

[46] The number of women graduates has been obtained in every case through the courtesy of the presidents of the colleges concerned. In some cases the women graduates have had to be selected from the total number of graduates and counted separately for the purpose. As the figures have never been printed before, I give them below: *22 colleges belonging to the Association of collegiate alumnæ*:—coeducational colleges: Boston, 522 graduates; California, 440; Chicago, 267; Cornell, 517; Kansas, 259; Leland Stanford, Jr., 289, Massachusetts institute technology, 45; Michigan, 940; Minnesota, 458; Nebraska, 263; Northwestern, 317; Oberlin, 1,486; Syracuse, 508; Wesleyan, 118; Wisconsin, 620. Independent colleges: Vassar, 1,509; Wellesley, 1,727; Smith, 1,679; Bryn Mawr, 321. Affiliated colleges: Radcliffe, 278; Barnard, 106; College for women of Western reserve, 135. *Additional colleges*, 15 in number: Women's college of Brown, 102; Cincinnati, 99; Columbian, 60; Colorado, about 70; Illinois, 131; Indiana, 282; Iowa, 340; Maine, 28; Missouri, no record; Ohio State university, 150; Ohio Wesleyan, 615; Texas, 60 Vanderbilt, 11; Washington (St. Louis), 55; West Virginia, 17. Total, 14,824 women graduates.

studied at universities, are very few;[47] in America, on the other hand, the higher education of women has assumed the proportions of a national movement still in progress. We may perhaps be able to guide in some degree its future development, but it has passed the experimental stage and can no longer be opposed with any hope of success. Its results are to be reckoned with as facts.

Health of college women[48]—Those who have come into contact with

[47] The number of women studying in universities in Germany in 1898–99 was approximately 471, probably mainly foreigners (statistics given in the Hochschul Nachrichten, Minerva, etc.); in France in 1896–97, approximately 410, of whom 83 were foreigners (Les Universités françaises, by M. Louis Liard; vol. 2 of Special Reports on Educational Subjects, Education department, London, 1898); in England and Wales in 1897–98, approximately 2,348. (See catalogues of different colleges.) The total number of women graduates in England and Wales who have received degrees, or their equivalent, from English and Welsh universities is about 2,180.

[48] Two statistical investigations of the health of college women have been undertaken; one in America in 1882, which tabulated various data connected with the health, occupation, marriage, birth rate, etc., of 705 graduates of the 12 American colleges belonging at that time to the Association of collegiate alumnæ (Health statistics of women college graduates; report of a special committee of the Association of collegiate alumnæ, Annie G. Howes, chairman; together with statistical tables collated by the Massachusetts bureau of statistics of labor. Boston: Wright and Potter Printing Co., 18 Post Office Square. 1885), and one in England in 1887 (Health statistics of women students of Cambridge and Oxford and of their sisters, by Mrs. Henry Sidgwick, Cambridge university press, 1890). The English statistics dealt with 566 women students (honor students who had taken tripos examinations and final honors, and women who had been in residence three, two and one year) of Newnham and Girton colleges, Cambridge, and of Lady Margaret and Somerville halls at Oxford. It was found that in England 75 per cent of the honor students were at the time of the investigation in excellent or good health. It was found that in America 78 per cent of the graduates were at the time of the investigation in good health and 5 per cent in fair health. In estimating the result of this investigation it is difficult to find a standard of comparison. There is no way of knowing what percentage of good health is to be expected in the case of the average woman who has not been to college. It is stated in the American health investigation, page 11, that Dr. Mary Putnam Jacobi, while obtaining data for her monograph on the question of rest for women, found that of 246 women only 56+ per cent were in good health. The American statistics were compared with the results obtained in an investigation of the condition of 1,032 working women of Boston, made by the Massachusetts bureau of statistics of labor; the comparison showed that the health of college women was more satisfactory than the health of working women. The English statistics were compared with the health statistics of 450 sisters or first cousins who had not received a college education, and it was found that, at all periods, about 5 per cent less of honor graduates were in bad health than of sisters and cousins. The comparative tables showed that the married graduates were healthier than their married sisters, that there were

some of the many thousands of healthy normal women studying in college at the present time, or who have had an opportunity to know something of the after-lives of even a small number of college women, believe that experience has proved them to be, both in college, and after leaving college, on the whole, in better physical condition than other women of the same age and social condition. Since, however, people who have not the opportunity of knowledge at first hand continue to regard the health of college women as a subject open for discussion, a new health investigation, based on questions sent to the 12,804 graduates of the 22 colleges belonging to the Association of collegiate alumnæ, is now in progress. The statistical tables will be collated a second time by the Massachusetts bureau of statistics of labor and sent to the Paris exposition as part of the educational exhibit of the Association of collegiate alumnæ.[49]

Marriage rate of college women—Here again no positive conclusions can be reached until we know what is the usual marriage rate of women belonging to the social class of women graduates. Everything indicates that the time of marriage is becoming later in the professional classes and that the marriage rate as a whole is decreasing. An investigation undertaken simultaneously with the new health investigation by the Association of collegiate alumnæ will enable us to speak with certainty in regard to the marriage rate of a large number of college women and their sisters.[50] It

fewer childless marriages among them, that they had a larger proportion of children per year of married life, and that their children were healthier.

[49] The health, marriage rate, birth rate, etc., of woman graduates will be compared in every case with the corresponding statistics for the women relatives nearest in age who have not received a college education; an attempt will also be made to obtain corresponding statistics for the nearest men relatives who are college graduates.

[50] The health investigation of English women students showed that the average age of marriage for students was 26.70 as against 25.53 for sisters, and that 10.25 per cent of the students were married and 19.33 per cent of the sisters, or, omitting the students who had just left college when the returns were sent in, about 12 per cent of students. The rate of marriage of students after their college course was completed and of their sisters seemed to be the same, the difference in the total number of marriages being apparently accounted for by causes existing before the termination of the college course, "possibly the desire to go to college, or to remain in college may be among them, but having been in college is not one of them." (See summary of results by Mrs. Sidgwick, page 59.) Mrs. Sidgwick concludes as a result of the investigation that not more than one-half of English women of the social class of women students or their sisters marry. The American investigation of 1883 showed that 27.8 per cent of the American college graduates, their average age being 28½ years, were at that time married, and that, judging by the indications of the marriage percentages among older graduates, about 50 per cent were likely sooner or later

must be borne in mind that the element of time is very important, and in the case of women the later and therefore younger classes are all larger than the earlier ones, see table on opposite page.

Occupations of college women—It is probable that about 50 per cent of women graduates teach for at least a certain number of years. Of the 705 women graduates whose occupations were reported in the Association of collegiate alumnæ investigation of 1883 50.2 percent were then teaching. In 1895 of 1,082 graduates of Vassar 37.7 per cent were teaching; 2.0 per cent were engaged in graduate study and 3.0 per cent were physicians or studying medicine. In 1898 of 171 graduates (all living) of Radcliffe college, including the class of 1898, 49.7 per cent were teaching; 8.7 per cent were engaged in graduate study; .6 per cent were studying medicine; 17.5 per cent were unmarried and without professional occupation. In 1899 of 316 living graduates of Bryn Mawr college, including the class of 1899, 39.0 percent were teaching; 11.4 were engaged in graduate study; 6 per cent were engaged in executive work (including 4 deans of colleges, 3 mistresses of college halls of residence); 1.6 per cent were studying or practising medicine, and 26.6 per cent were unmarried and without professional occupation.[51]

to be married. In an investigation of the marriage of Vassar graduates made in 1895, and not including the graduates of that year, it was found that rather under 38 per cent of the whole number of students, and about 63 per cent of the first four classes, were married, see Frances M. Abbott: A Generation of college women, The Forum, vol. XX, p. 378. Out of the total number of 8,956 graduates, including those graduating in June, 1899, of the 16 colleges belonging to the Association of collegiate alumnæ that have kept accurate marriage statistics, 2,059 are married, or 23.0 per cent.

[51] Mrs. Sidgwick's investigation showed that 77 per cent of all English students reporting, and 83 per cent of honor students, had engaged in educational work.

<table>
<tr><th colspan="3">Marriage rate of college women</th></tr>
<tr><th></th><th>Opened in</th><th>Percentage of graduates married</th></tr>
<tr><td>Vassar</td><td>1865</td><td>35.1</td></tr>
<tr><td>Kansas</td><td>1866</td><td>31.3</td></tr>
<tr><td>Minnesota</td><td>1868</td><td>24.5</td></tr>
<tr><td>Cornell</td><td rowspan="3">1870</td><td rowspan="3">31.0</td></tr>
<tr><td>Syracuse</td></tr>
<tr><td>Wesleyan</td></tr>
<tr><td>Nebraska</td><td>1871</td><td>24.3</td></tr>
<tr><td>Boston</td><td>1873</td><td>22.2</td></tr>
<tr><td>Wellesley</td><td rowspan="2">1875</td><td rowspan="2">18.4</td></tr>
<tr><td>Smith</td></tr>
<tr><td>Radcliffe</td><td>1879</td><td>16.5</td></tr>
<tr><td>Bryn Mawr</td><td>1885</td><td>15.2</td></tr>
<tr><td>Barnard</td><td>1889</td><td>10.4</td></tr>
<tr><td>Leland Stanford Junior</td><td>1891</td><td>9.7</td></tr>
<tr><td>Chicago</td><td>1892</td><td>9.4</td></tr>
</table>

It will be seen that independent, affiliated and coeducational colleges fall into their proper place in the series, thus showing conclusively that the method of obtaining a college education exercises scarcely any appreciable influence on the marriage rate.

The marriage rate of Bryn Mawr college, calculated in January, 1900, will also serve as an illustration of the importance of time in every consideration of the marriage rate: graduates of the class of 1889, married, 40.7 per cent; graduates of the first two classes, 1889–1890, married, 40.0 per cent; graduates of the first three classes, 1889–1891, married, 33.3 per cent; graduates of the first four classes, 1889–1892, married, 32.9 per cent; graduates of the first five classes, 1889–1893, married, 31.0 per cent; graduates of the first six classes, 1889–1894, married, 30.0 per cent; graduates of the first seven classes, 1889–1895, married, 25.2 per cent; graduates of the first eight classes, 1889–1896, married, 22.8 per cent; graduates of the first nine classes, 1889–1897, married, 20.9 per cent; graduates of the first ten classes, 1889–1898, married, 17.2 per cent; graduates of the first eleven classes, 1889–1899, married, 15.2 per cent.

Coeducation vs. separate education—It is clear that coeducation is the prevailing method in the United States; it is the most economical method; indeed it is the only possible method in most parts of the country. Now that it has been determined in America to send girls as well as boys to college, it becomes impossible to duplicate colleges for women in every part of this vast country. If, as is shown by the statistics given in the successive reports of the commissioner of education, men students in college are increasing faster far than the ratio of the population, and women college students are increasing faster still than men,[52] it will tax all our resources to make adequate provision for men and women in common. Only in thickly-settled parts of the country, where public sentiment is conservative enough to justify the initial outlay, have separate colleges for women been established, and these colleges, without exception, have been private foundations. Public opinion in the United States almost universally demands that universities supported by public taxation should provide for the college education of the women of the state in which they are situated. The separate colleges for women speaking generally are to be found almost exclusively in the narrow strip of colonial states lying along the Atlantic seaboard. The question is often asked, whether women prefer coeducation or separate education. It seems that in the east they as yet prefer separate education, and this preference is natural.[53] College life as it is organized in a woman's college seems to conservative parents less exposed, more in accordance with inherited traditions. Consequently, girls who in their own homes lead guarded lives,

[52] Between 1890 and 1898 women undergraduate students have increased 111.8 per cent, and men undergraduate students have increased 51.2 per cent.

[53] In the college departments of coeducational colleges the average number of women studying is 48.4, whereas in the college departments of independent women's colleges the average number of women studying is 331.91, and in affiliated colleges 192.8. In 1897–98 11.4 per cent of all the women studying in coeducational colleges obtained the bachelor's degree, whereas 13.4 per cent of all the women studying in independent women's colleges obtained the bachelor's degree, which indicates probably that women prefer women's colleges for four years of residence. In the same year 13.3 per cent of all men undergraduate students obtained the bachelor's degree. The average number of graduates of the 4 women's colleges belonging to the Association of collegiate alumnæ is 1,309 per college, the average age of the colleges being 23 years; the average number of graduates of the 15 coeducational colleges belonging to the Association of college alumnæ is only 469.9, although the average age of the colleges is 27.7 years. During the 8 years from 1890 to 1898, women undergraduate students have increased in coeducational colleges 105.4 per cent, whereas they have increased in women's colleges, division A, 138.4 per cent. Precisely the reverse is true of men students (see pp. 15 and 16, including foot notes).

are to be found rather in women's colleges than in coeducational colleges. From the point of view of conservative parents, there is undoubtedly serious objection to intimate association at the most impressionable period of a girl's life with many young men from all parts of the country and of every possible social class. From every point of view it is undesirable to have the problems of love and marriage presented for decision to a young girl during the four years when she ought to devote her energies to profiting by the only systematic intellectual training she is likely to receive during her life. Then, too, for the present, much of the culture and many of the priceless associations of college life are to be obtained, whether for men or women, only by residence in college halls, and no coeducational, or even affiliated, colleges have as yet organized for their students such a complete college life as the independent woman's college. So long as this preference, and the grounds for it, exist, we must see to it that separate colleges for women are no less good than colleges for men. In professional schools, including the graduate school of the faculty of philosophy, coeducation is even at present almost the only method. There are in the United States only 4 true graduate schools for men closed to women, and only 1 independent graduate school maintained for women offering three years' consecutive work leading to the degree of Ph. D. There is every reason to believe that as soon as large numbers of women wish to enter upon the study of theology, law and medicine, all the professional schools now existing will become coeducational.

A modified vs. an unmodified curriculum—The progress of women's education, as we have traced it briefly from its beginning in the coeducational college of Oberlin in 1833, and the independent woman's college of Vassar in 1865, has been a progress in accordance with the best academic traditions of men's education. In 1870 we could not have predicted the course to be taken by the higher education of women; the separate colleges for women might have developed into something wholly different from what we had been familiar with so long in the separate colleges for men. A female course in coeducational colleges in which music and art were substituted for mathematics and Greek might have met the needs of the women students. After thirty years of experience, however, we are prepared to say that whatever changes may be made in future in the college curriculum will be made for men and women alike. After all, women themselves must be permitted to be the judges of what kind of intellectual discipline they find most truly serviceable. They seem to have made up their minds, and hereafter may be trusted to see to it that an inferior education shall not be offered to them in women's colleges, or elsewhere, under the name of a modified curriculum.

Printed by Libri Plureos GmbH in Hamburg,
Germany